Little Pebble™

Baby Animals and Their Homes

BABY ANIMALS In DENS

by Martha E. H. Rustad

CAPSTONE PRESS
a capstone imprint

Little Pebble is published by Capstone Press,
1710 Roe Crest Drive, North Mankato, Minnesota 56003
www.mycapstone.com

Library of Congress Cataloging-in-Publication Data
Names: Rustad, Martha E. H. (Martha Elizabeth Hillman), 1975- author.
Title: Baby animals in dens / by Martha E. H. Rustad.
Description: North Mankato, Minnesota : Capstone Press, [2017] | Series:
     Little pebble. Baby animals and their homes | Audience: Ages 4-8. |
Audience: K to grade 3. | Includes bibliographical references and index.
Identifiers: LCCN 2016031960| ISBN 9781515738305 (library binding)
     ISBN 9781515738343 (pbk.) | ISBN 9781515738466 (ebook pdf)
Subjects: LCSH: Animals—Habitations—Juvenile literature. |
     Animals—Infancy—Juvenile literature.
Classification: LCC QL756 .R87 2017 | DDC 591.56/4—dc23
LC record available at https://lccn.loc.gov/2016031960

Editorial Credits
Carrie Braulick Sheely, editor; Juliette Peters, designer;
Tracey Engel, media researcher; Katy LaVigne, production specialist

Photo Credits
Alamy: Rick & Nora Bowers, 8–9, WILDLIFE GmbH, 21; Getty Images: D. Robert & Lorri Franz, 4–5, Thorsten Milse/robertharding, 13; National Geographic Creative: DES & JEN BARTLETT, 17; Newscom: Dave Watts/NHPA/Photoshot, 6–7; NHPA: Photoshot/Gerard Lacz, Front Cover; Shutterstock: Ales Liska, Back Cover and Interior Design Element, Brad Sauter, 1 Bottom Left, David Rasmus, 11, Geoffrey Kuchera, 19, sittipong, Back Cover Design Element, Tony Moran, 3 Bottom Left; Visuals Unlimited: Steve Maslowski, 15

Printed and bound in China.
007873

Table of Contents

Dens High and Low

Some baby animals grow up in dens. Dens hide them from other animals.

Dig!

A coyote digs a den.

She has cubs.

They stay warm.

Ocelot kittens have
dark spots.
They stay close to mom.
Purr!

Two bear cubs share a den.

It is in a cave.

They drink milk from mom.

A polar bear den

is in snow.

Cubs peek out.

This den is in a tree.

New raccoon babies

can't see.

Mom keeps them safe.

Growing Up

Beaver kits live in dens.

The opening is underwater.

They swim out.

Splash!

Older fox cubs go out.

Sniff! They hunt for mice.

A red panda picks up
her cub.

She finds a new den.

Dens make good homes.

Glossary

cub—the young of coyotes, foxes, bears, pandas, and some other animals

den—a home for some animals; a den may be in a cave, hollow log, or other sheltered place

hunt—to find and kill animals for food

kit—the young of beavers, raccoons, and some other animals

ocelot—a wildcat that lives mainly in Central and South America

Read More

Lake, G.G. *Red Foxes.* Woodland Wildlife. North Mankato, Minn.: Capstone, 2017.

Marsh, Laura. *Polar Bears.* National Geographic Readers. Washington, D.C.: National Geographic, 2013.

Wilson, Emily. *Inside Beaver Lodges.* Inside Animal Homes. New York: PowerKids Press, 2016.

Internet Sites

FactHound offers a safe, fun way to find Internet sites related to this book. All of the sites on FactHound have been researched by our staff.

Here's all you do:
Visit *www.facthound.com*
Type in this code: 9781515738305

Check out projects, games and lots more at
www.capstonekids.com

Critical Thinking Using the Common Core

1. Look at the picture on page 9. Why do you think the kittens have darker spots than the mother? How can this coloring help the kittens stay safe? (Craft and Structure)

2. Red pandas move their cubs to new dens often. Why do you think they do this? (Integration of Knowledge and Ideas)

Index